VIOLA

TEAM STRINGS

CHRISTOPHER BULL
OLIVE GOODBORN &
RICHARD DUCKETT

International Music Publications Limited

Edited by BARRIE CARSON TURNER

Piano accompaniments by CHRISTOPHER BULL

INTERNATIONAL MUSIC PUBLICATIONS LIMITED would like to thank the following publishers for permission to use arrangements of their copyright material in TEAM STRINGS.

Sincere thanks are extended to the following people:
ANN GOODBORN, Double Bass Tutor, Birmingham Schools Symphony Orchestra, for her invaluable advice on technical matters.
ANGELA GREGORY of Kings Norton Girls School, Birmingham, and all the pupils who worked on the material in preparation.

First Published 1993.

Cover Design: IAN BARRETT
Cover Photography: RON GOLDBY
Production: STEPHEN CLARK and MARK MUMFORD
Typesetting: Headline Publicity Ltd., Chelmsford, Essex
Instruments photographed are "Andreas Zeller" courtesy of Stentor Music Co. Ltd., Reigate, England.
Printed in England by Halstan & Co. Ltd., Amersham, Bucks.

TEAM STRINGS: Viola
ISBN 0 86359 987 7/ORDER REF: 18416/215-2-878

Team Strings Ensemble

TEAM STRINGS ensemble material has been specially written so that it can be played by almost any combination of string instruments the teacher may encounter.

On each ensemble page there are three parts. The first is the melody and the second is a duet part. The third is either a bass line, a harmony part or a descant. Each piece can therefore be used as a solo, duet, or trio, with or without piano accompaniment.

By allocating the parts to different instruments it is easy to create a considerable variety of mixed ensembles, from a simple duet to a full string orchestra.

In addition to this, each piece can be extended into a longer one by varying the textures in subsequent verses. This can be done by reallocating the parts, playing in unison, using *pizzicato* accompaniments, introducing solo passages, etc.

The following symbols have been used to provide an immediate visual identification:

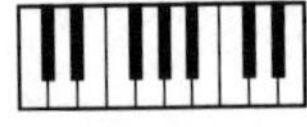 Pieces with piano accompaniment

 Ensemble page
(score included in ACCOMPANIMENTS book)

□ Pieces which appear in the same place on the same page in all four TEAM STRINGS books.

Introducing Team Strings

The TEAM STRINGS series has been designed to meet the needs of young string players everywhere, whether lessons are given individually, in groups or in the classroom.

Musical variety

Each book contains a wide variety of musical styles, from the Baroque and Classical eras to Christmas carols, folk music, and popular favourites. In addition there are many original pieces, studies and technical exercises. Furthermore, TEAM STRINGS offers material for mixed string ensemble as well as solos with piano accompaniment.

Ensemble pieces

All TEAM STRINGS books contain corresponding pages of music which can be played together in harmony. Thus, even beginners are given early ensemble experience and the opportunity to share lessons with other players.

Every TEAM STRINGS book contains a supplement relating to the duets in TEAM WOODWIND for flute and oboe. There are also string parts which can be used in conjunction with TEAM BRASS, TEAM WOODWIND and TEAM PERCUSSION to form mixed instrumental ensembles.

National Curriculum & GCSE skills

TEAM STRINGS has been designed to help meet the requirements of the National Curriculum for music. In addition to fostering musical literacy, 'Rhythm Grids' and 'Play By Ear' lines provide early opportunities for composition and improvisation. This aspect of TEAM STRINGS can be a useful starting point for these elements in the GCSE examination course now followed by most secondary schools.

Comprehensive notes on the use of this series, scores of the ensemble material, piano accompaniments and approaches to creative music making are given in the ACCOMPANIMENTS book.

Supplementary Material

Parts are available for Brass, Woodwind, Recorder and Percussion which can be added to the TEAM STRINGS ensembles. Each piece can therefore be extended to incorporate a wide variety of additional instruments. These supplementary parts can be used for almost any combination of instruments from a small '*ad hoc*' group to full orchestra.

Wind, Brass, and Percussion parts for the Ensemble Pieces in TEAM STRINGS are available separately.

Lesson diary & practice chart

Date (week commencing)	Enter number of minutes practised.							Teacher indicates which pages to study.
	Mon	Tue	Wed	Thur	Fri	Sat	Sun	

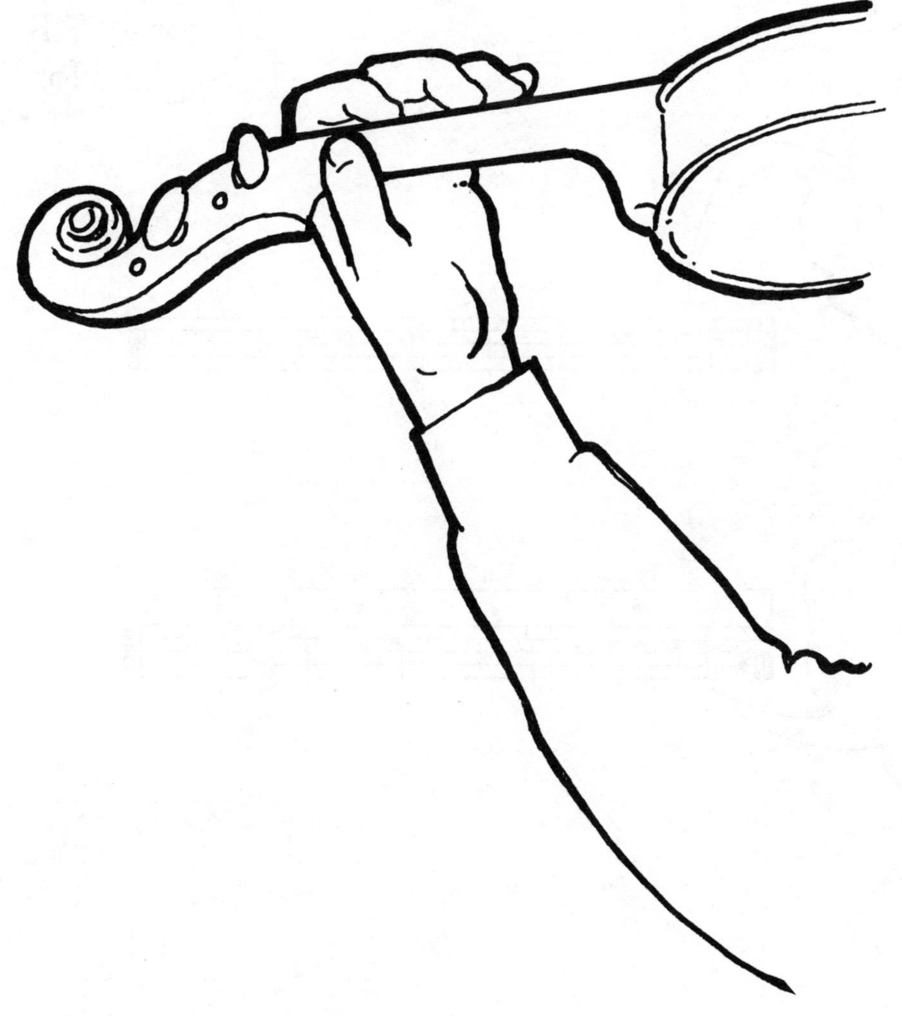

Start with D . . .

*French time-names may be used.

. . . then on to A

0
Clap, say, and play the rhythm
A CROTCHET REST lasts for ONE beat
Open A is written above the top line
BAR LINES divide a line of notes into sets. In 4/4 time each bar adds up to four crotchet beats
1+1+1+1= 4
2+2= 4

D and A together

A MINIM rest lasts for two beats

Find the A string with your finger during the rests

Music is written on a set of five lines and four spaces called a STAVE

By the Rhine

This piece fits with *German tune* (page 23).

The note G

G and D together

A little march

Chiming bells

G, D and A

The note C

A lively piece

All four strings

Barn dance

Starlight

This pieces fits with *Twinkle, twinkle little star* (page 27).

On the lake

This piece fits with *Flamingo* (page 12).

The traveller

This piece fits with *Tramping* (page 11).

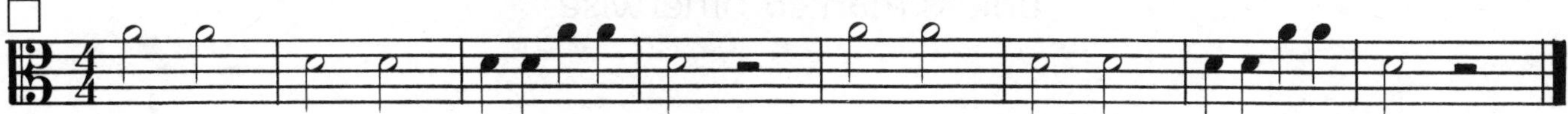

The pendulum

This piece fits with *The clock* (page 15).

At dusk

This piece fits with *Now the day is over* (page 19).

Magic spells

This piece fits with *The wizard* (page 43).

Using the bow

Down bow

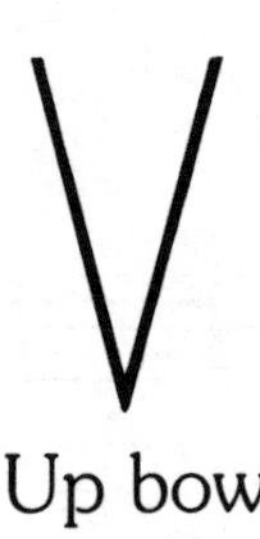

Up bow

ARCO means play with the bow.

PIZZICATO (or *pizz*) means pluck the strings.

From now on everything can be played *arco*, unless marked otherwise.

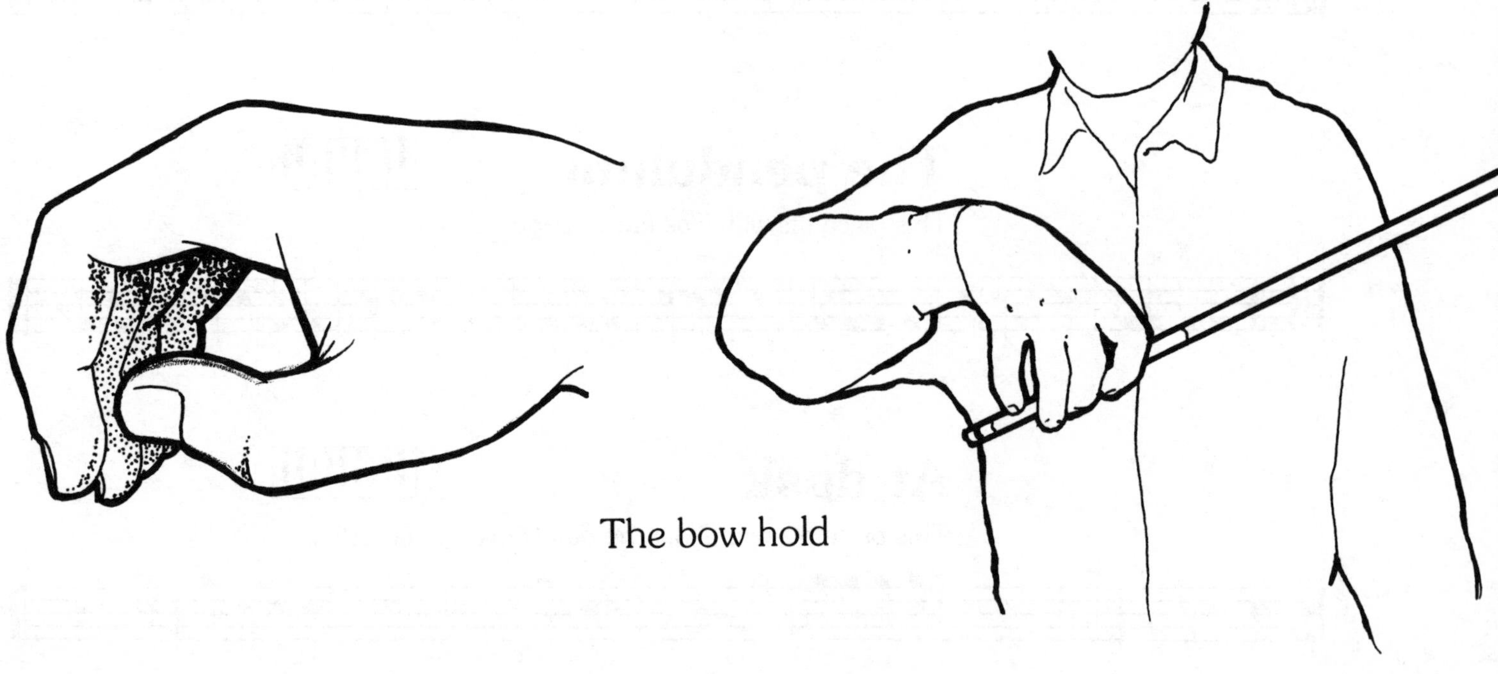

The bow hold

Bowing exercises

■ The music on pages 2 - 7 can also be used as bowing exercises.

First finger E

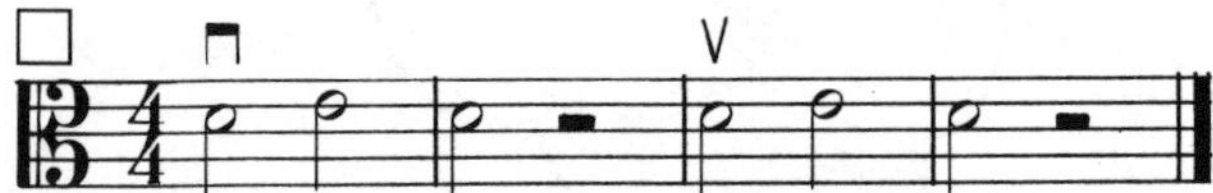

By the stream

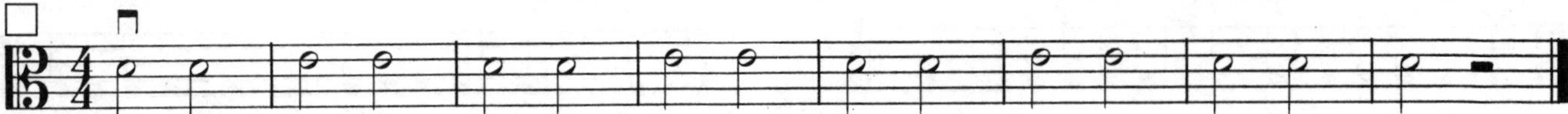

The night sky

This piece fits with *Twinkle, twinkle little star* (page 27).

Second finger F♯

Down bow

Tramping

Traditional

The sharp sign makes all the notes in the bar with the same letter name sharp

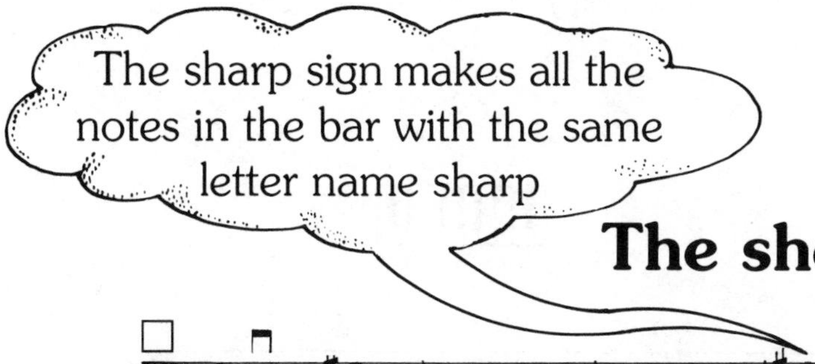

The shepherd

Bavaria

This piece fits with *German tune* (page 23).

Third finger G

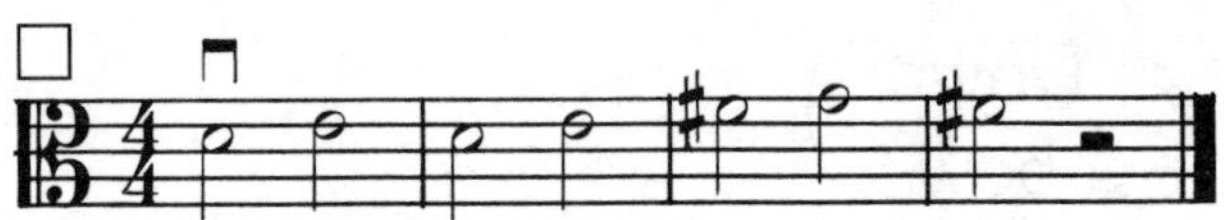

Flamingo  

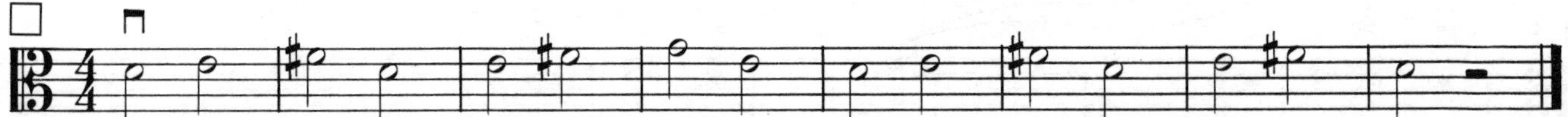

The magic carpet 

This piece fits with *The wizard* (page 43).

Tunes using D E F♯ & G

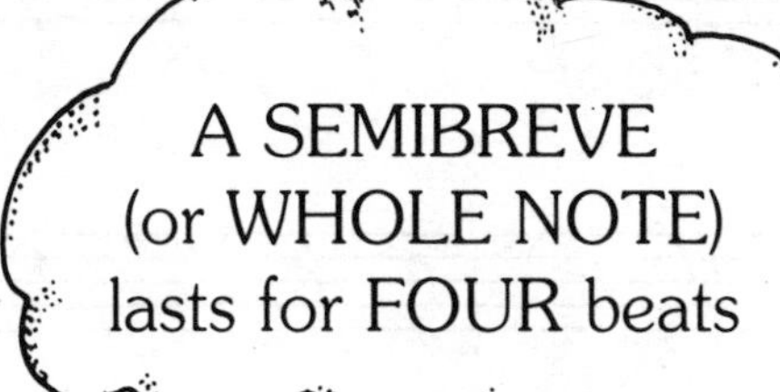

The piper

Lucy

Folk song

Falling leaves

This piece fits with *Autumn* (page 21).

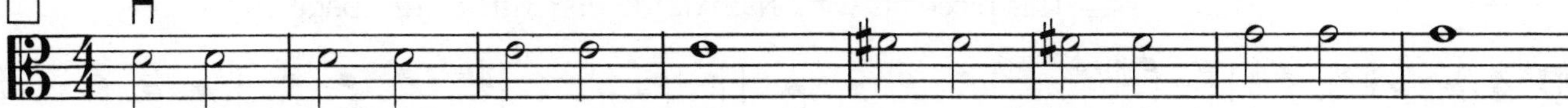

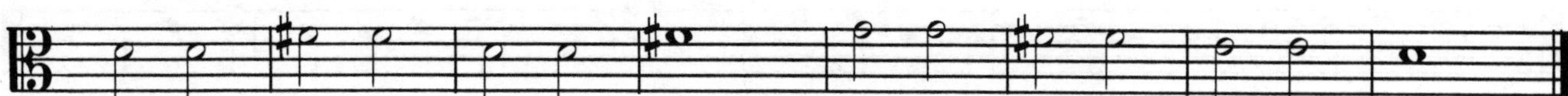

Gospel song

This piece fits with *All night, all day* (page 51).

Kingston

This piece fits with *Jamaican dance* (page 49).

Coronation march

This piece fits with *Procession* (page 25).

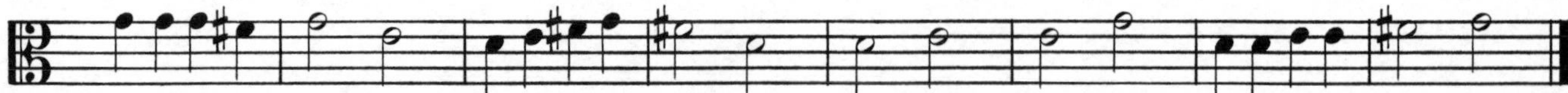

The astronomer

This piece fits with *Twinkle, twinkle little star* (page 27).

Notes on the G string

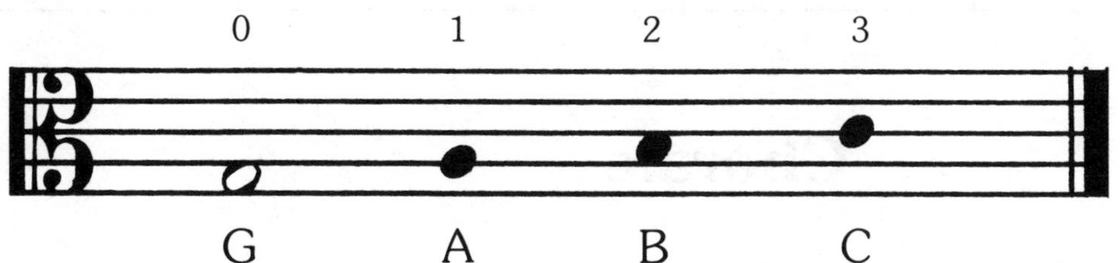

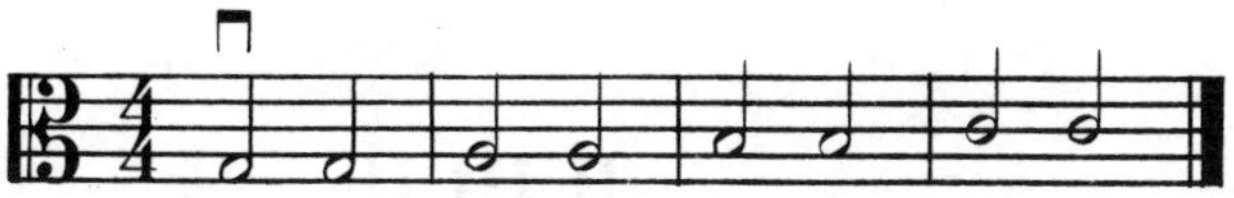

Merrily we roll along

Traditional

On parade

The clock

In the belfry

Pennyroyal

Chorale

Scottish air

Rutland

The grasshopper

Notes on the A string

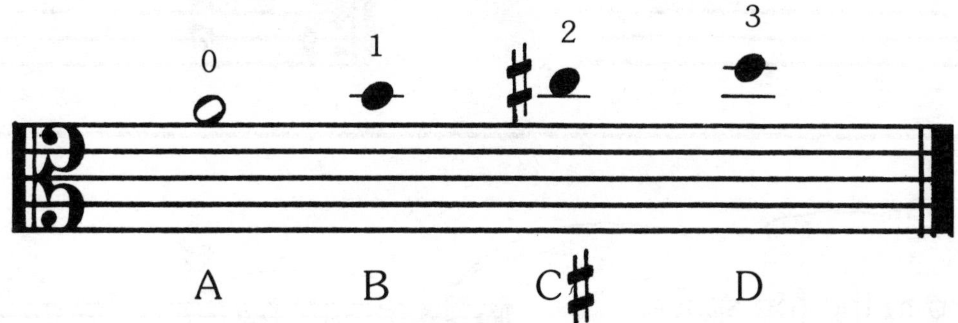

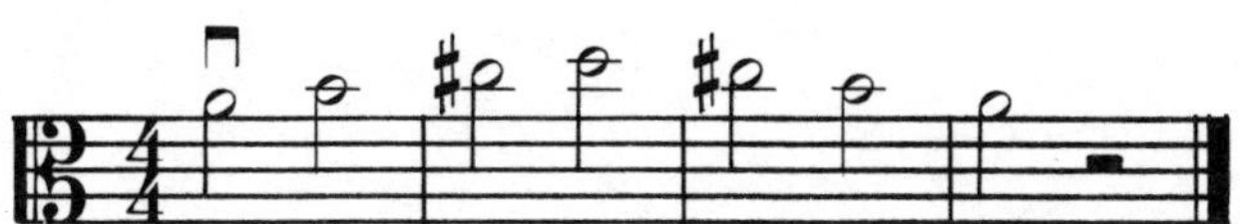

The harvest

Au clair de la lune

French traditional

Make up your own piece using the notes on the A string

Dance

The key signature of G

The key signature of D

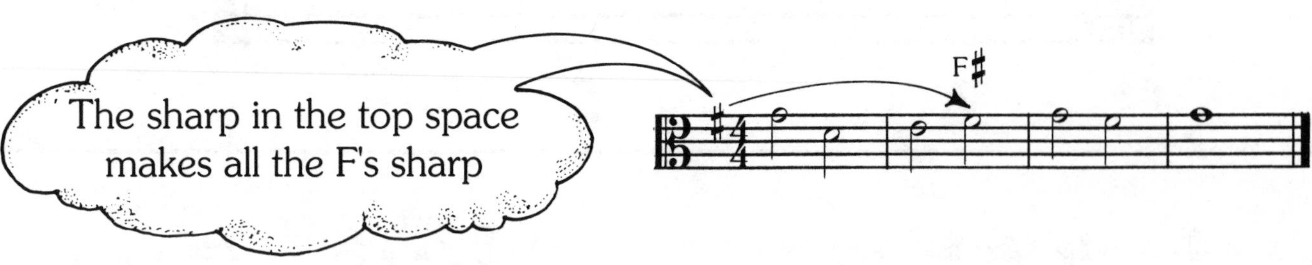

Promenade

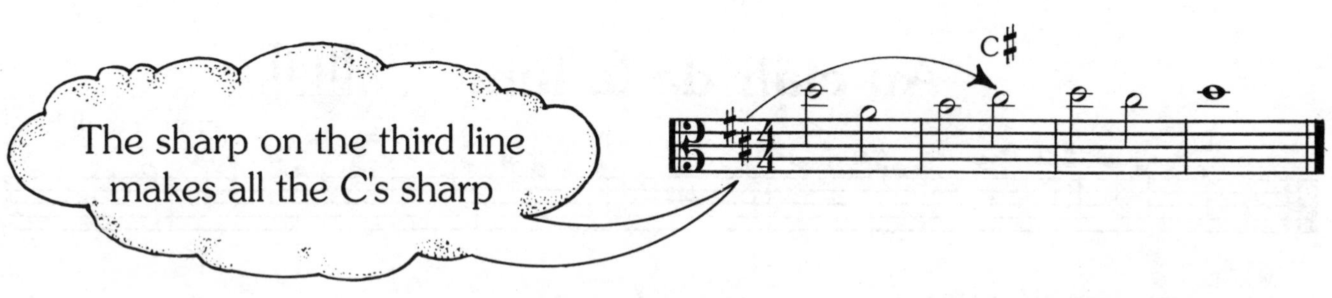

Daydreams

Five-note patterns

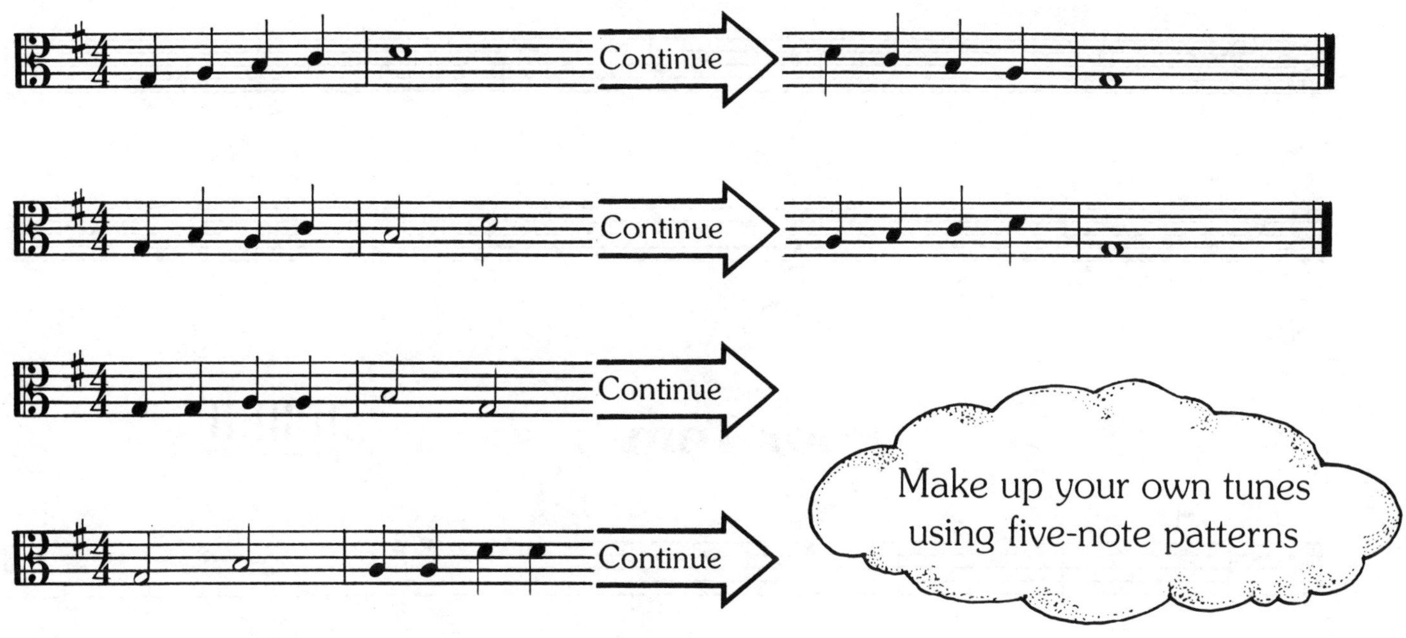

Now the day is over

S. BARING-GOULD (1834-1924)

Quick march

Mr Foster's round

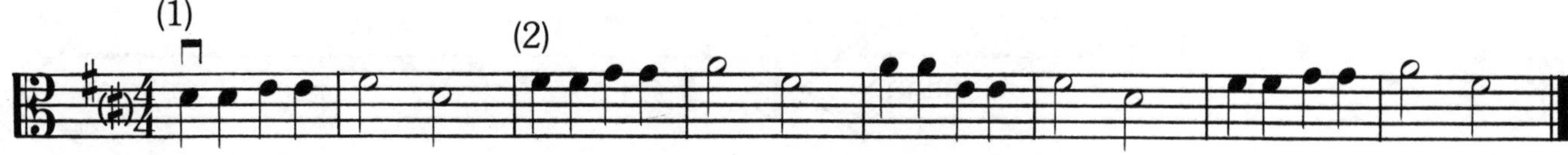

Chinese lantern

Poor Tom

Duet

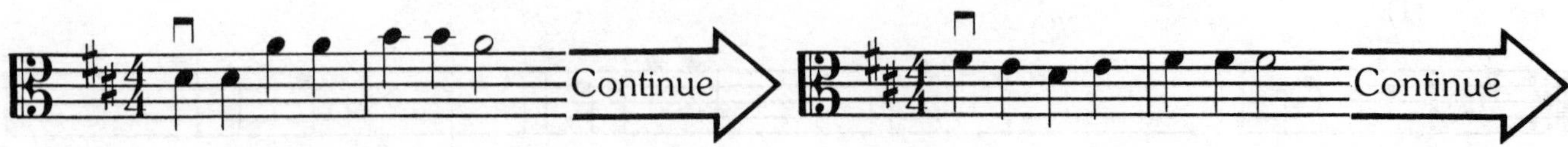

Autumn

1.
Adding the second part turns *Autumn* into a DUET
2.
All three parts played together make a TRIO
3.

Dotted minims

Sorrow

Rigaudon

HENRY PURCELL (1658-1695)

Arpeggios

Shady grove

American traditional

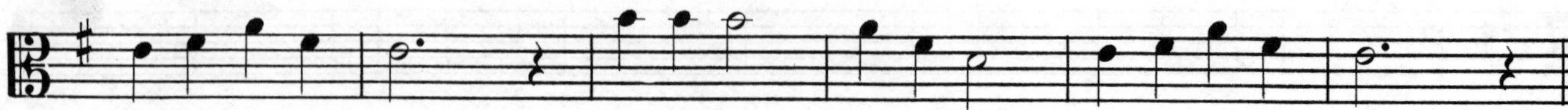

German tune

Traditional

1.

2.

3.

Quavers

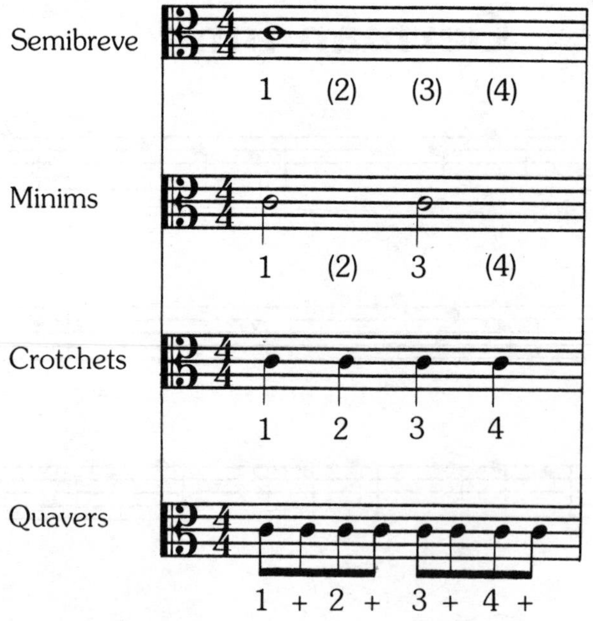

Semibreve

1 (2) (3) (4)

Minims

1 (2) 3 (4)

Crotchets

1 2 3 4

Quavers

1 + 2 + 3 + 4 +

Each bar adds up to four crotchets

Two QUAVERS (or EIGHTH NOTES) ♪ ♪ or ♫ add up to one crotchet

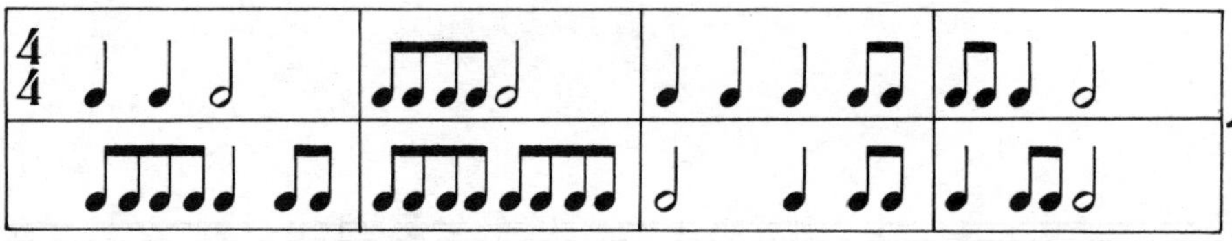

Clap, say, and play the rhythm

My goose

Round

Procession

This old man

English traditional

Round go the mill wheels

French traditional

One player only

Everyone together

Song and dance

West Indian traditional

Solo Tutti Solo

Tutti Solo Tutti

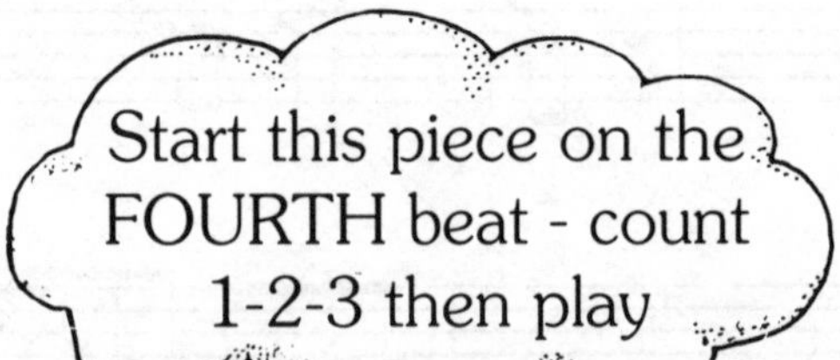

Solo Tutti

Start this piece on the FOURTH beat - count 1-2-3 then play

Popular song

American traditional

Twinkle, twinkle little star

Traditional

'Swops'

Duet

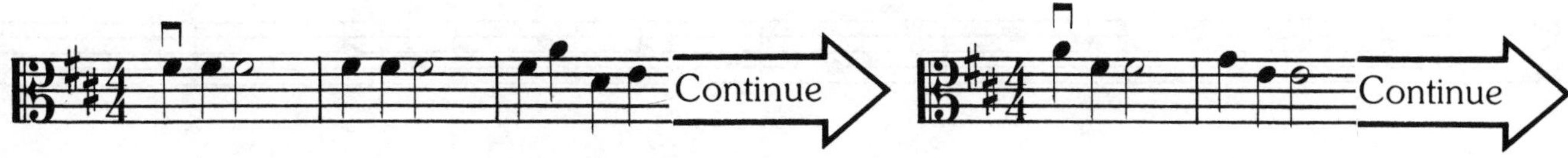

Little donkey

Words and Music by
ERIC BOSWELL

Okushiri

Japanese traditional

Kol dodi

Jewish traditional

Russian lullaby

Go tell Aunt Rhody

American traditional

Magnolia

Long, long ago

T. H. BAYLY

Composing your own music

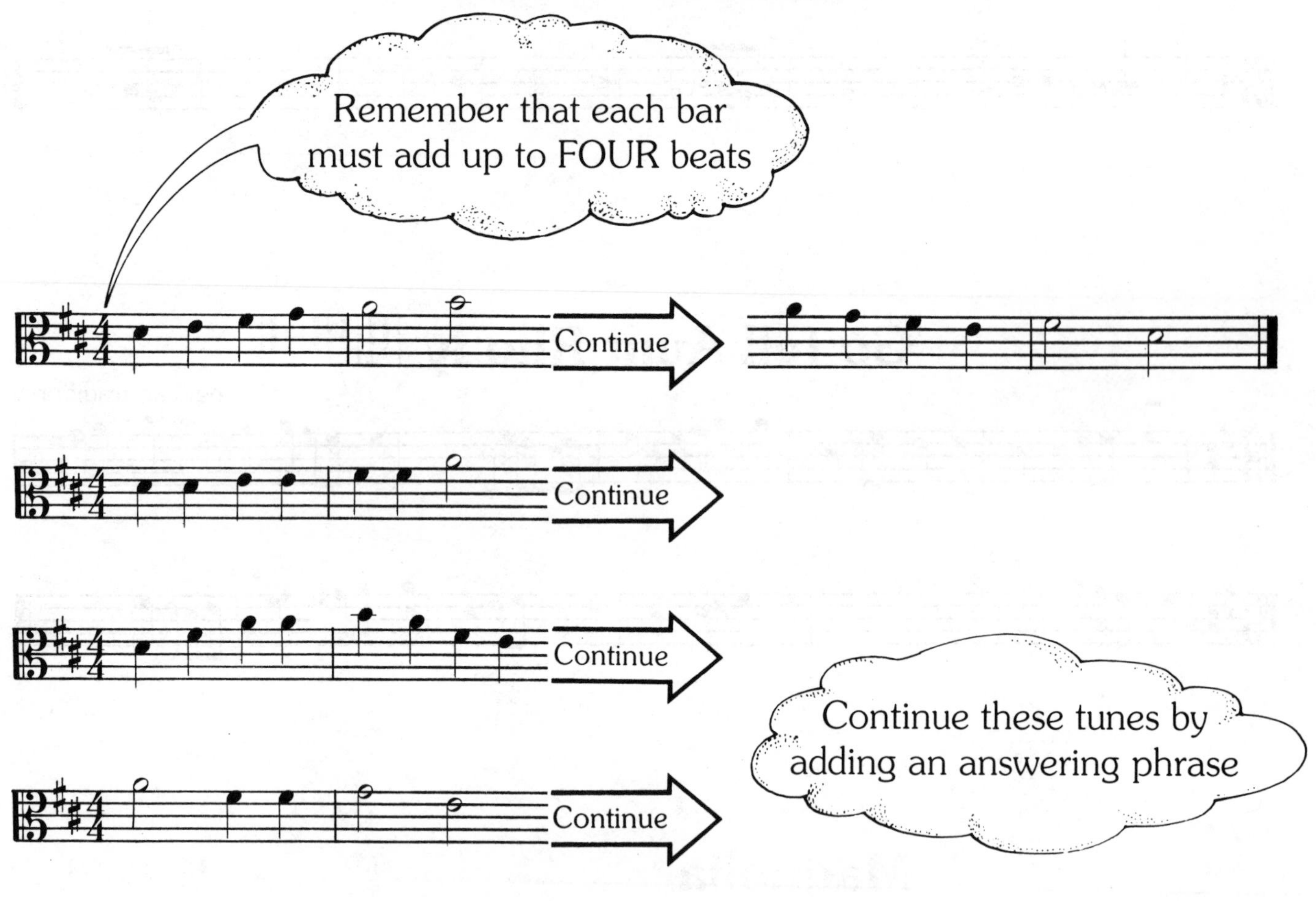

Round

Workin' on the railroad

SUPPLEMENT

International Music Publications Limited

German tune

Ensemble part for TEAM WOODWIND version in F.

Traditional

Lullaby

Ensemble part for TEAM WOODWIND version in F.

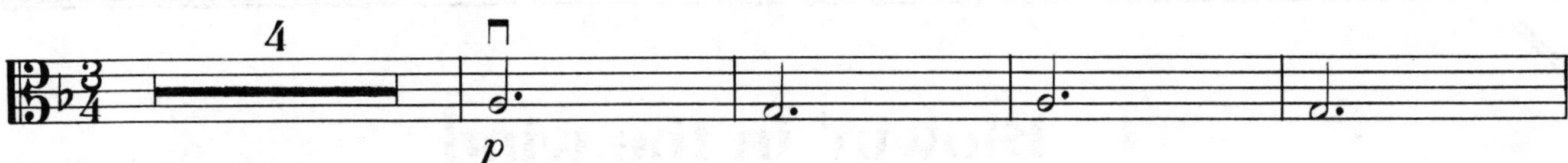

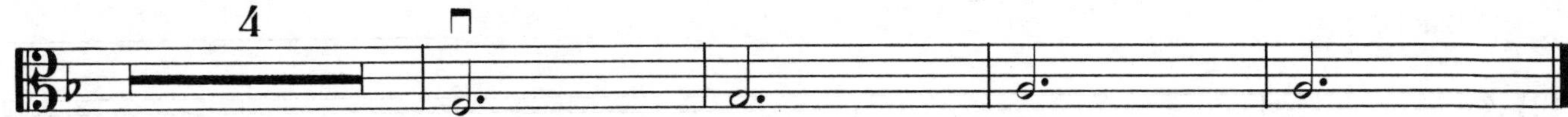

Regal fanfare

Ensemble part for TEAM WOODWIND version in G.

Maestoso

21

When I first came to this land

Ensemble part for TEAM WOODWIND version in F.

27

Blowin' in the wind

Ensemble part for TEAM WOODWIND version in C.

Words and music by BOB DYLAN

Steadily

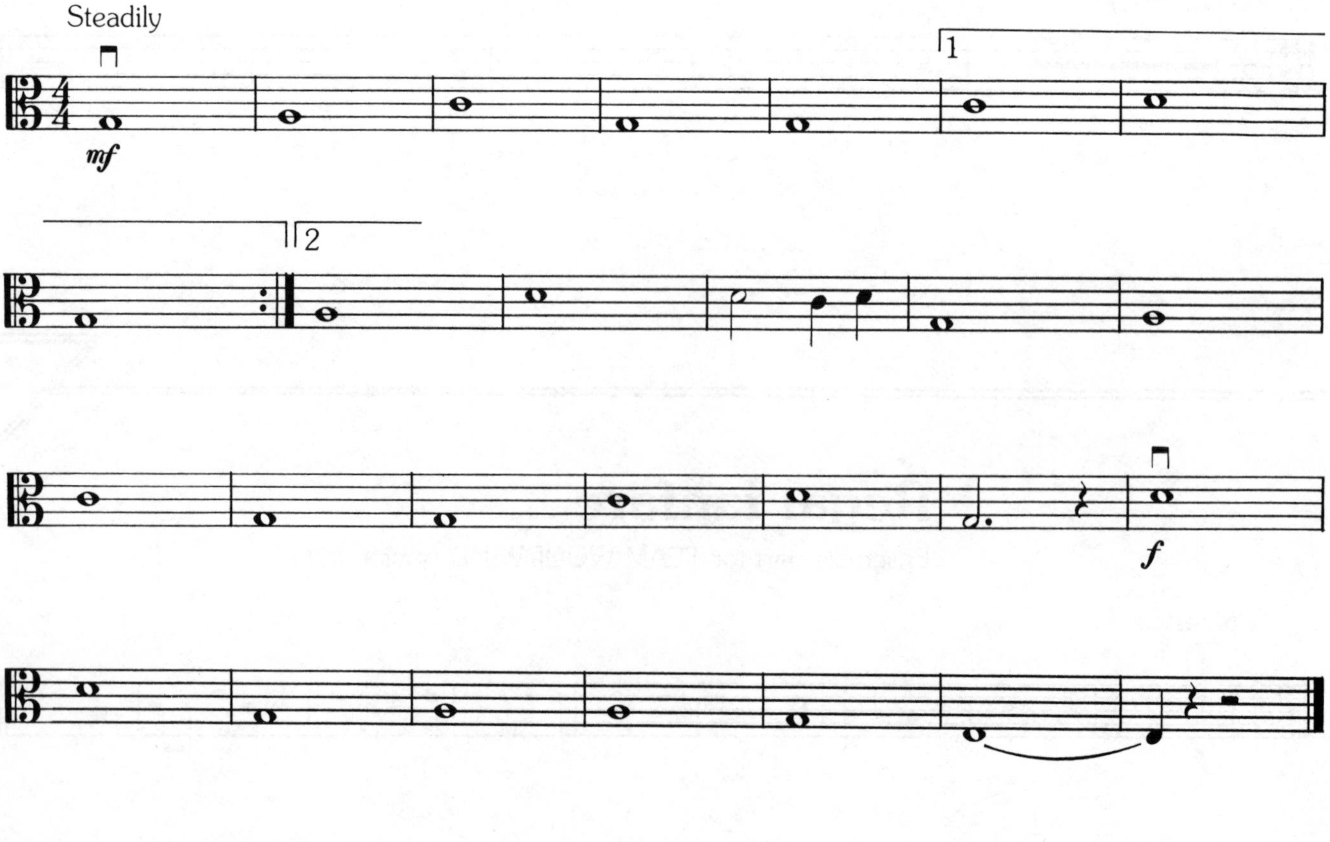

German tune

Ensemble part for TEAM BRASS/WOODWIND version in B♭.

Traditional

Lullaby

Ensemble part for TEAM BRASS/WOODWIND version in B♭.

Regal fanfare

Ensemble part for TEAM BRASS/WOODWIND version in B♭.

Maestoso

When I first came to this land

Ensemble part for TEAM BRASS/WOODWIND version in B♭.

Traditional

Blowin' in the wind

Ensemble part for TEAM BRASS/WOODWIND version in B♭.

Words and music by BOB DYLAN

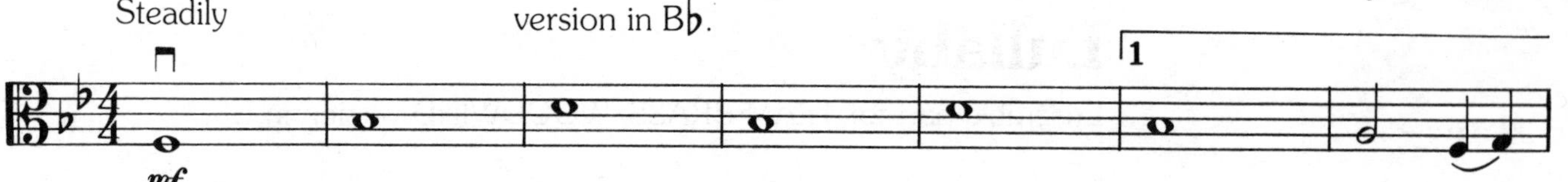

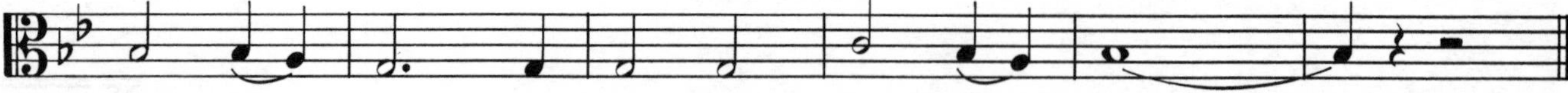

Au clair de la lune

French traditional

Ensemble part for TEAM BRASS/WOODWIND version in F.

37

Little donkey

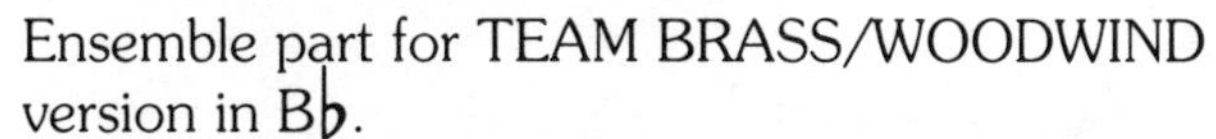

Ensemble part for TEAM BRASS/WOODWIND version in B♭.

Words and music by ERIC BOSWELL

39

Tijuana brass

Ensemble part for TEAM BRASS/WOODWIND version in E♭.

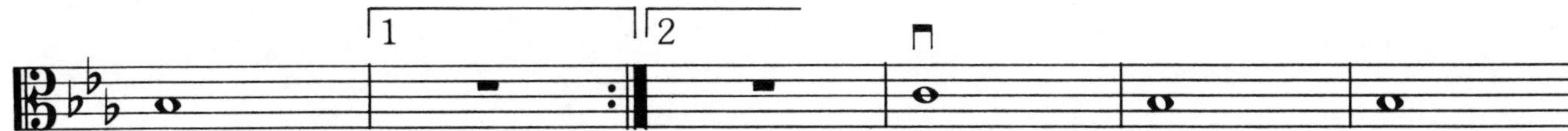

I saw three ships

Ensemble part for TEAM BRASS/WOODWIND version in E♭.

Traditional

48

Michael row the boat ashore

Ensemble part for TEAM BRASS/WOODWIND version in B♭.

Spiritual

Notes on the C string

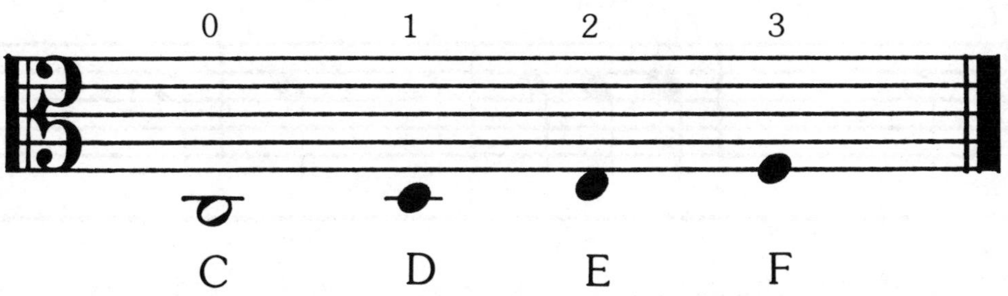

Cowboy song

Ozibani

Tribal song from Zambia

Welcome spring

Swiss traditional

Hide and seek

German traditional

3/4 time

Waltz

Going home

Blow the wind southerly

English traditional

Chanson

Eliza

Past three o'clock

Oranges and lemons

London's burning

Round

English traditional

(1) (2) (3) (4)

Ye banks and braes

Scottish traditional

A handsome lad

Irish traditional

Congratulations

Words and Music by
BILL MARTIN and PHIL COULTER

Minuet

WOLFGANG AMADEUS MOZART
(1756-1791)

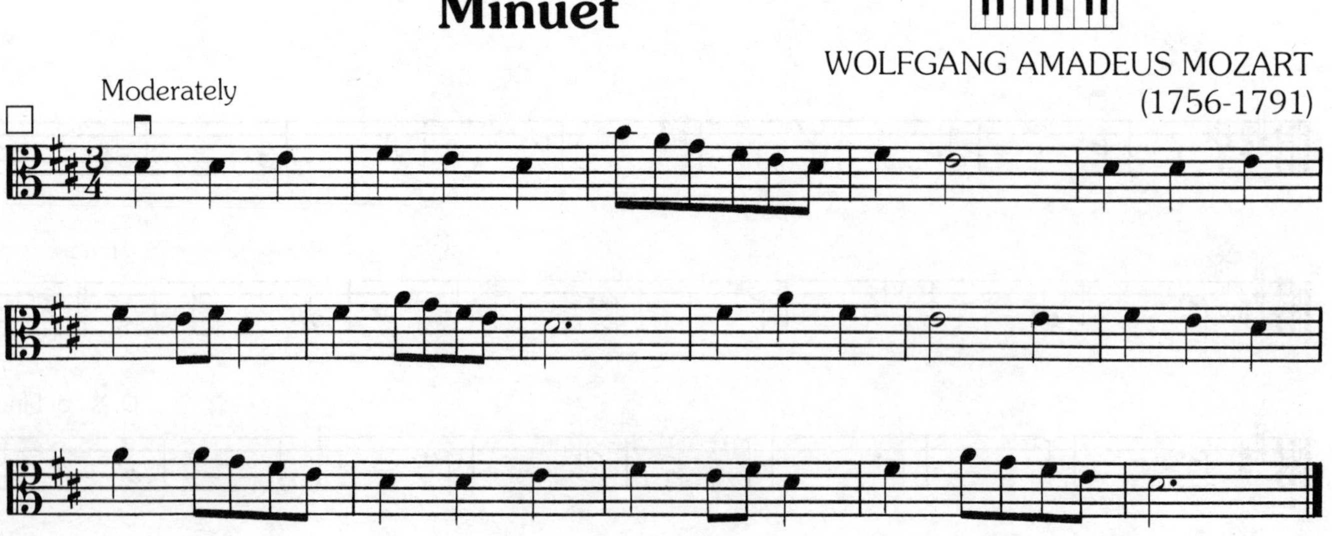

Mongoose
Brightly
Jamaican traditional
Up bow
The prospector
Steadily
American traditional
Schottisch
FRANZ SCHUBERT
(1797-1828)
Simply
Now we are met
Slowly
Duet

Dotted crotchets

Michael row the boat ashore

Moderately

Spiritual

The muffin man

English traditional

Rhythmically

Village song

Not too fast

Peruvian traditional

Kum ba yah

Spiritual

Edelweiss

From *The Sound of Music*

Lyrics by OSCAR HAMMERSTEIN II
Music by RICHARD RODGERS

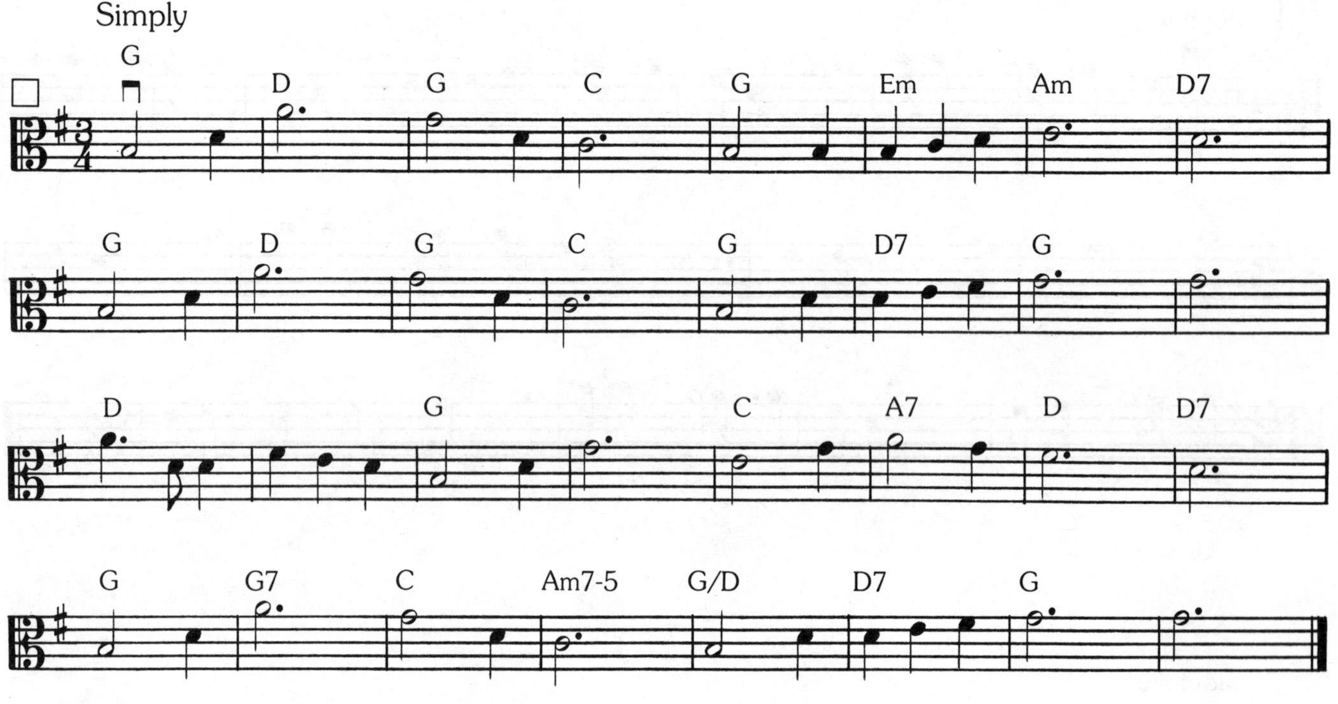

London bridge

English traditional

Donkey riding

Traditional

Music for viols

Paloma blanca

Words and Music by
J BOUWENS

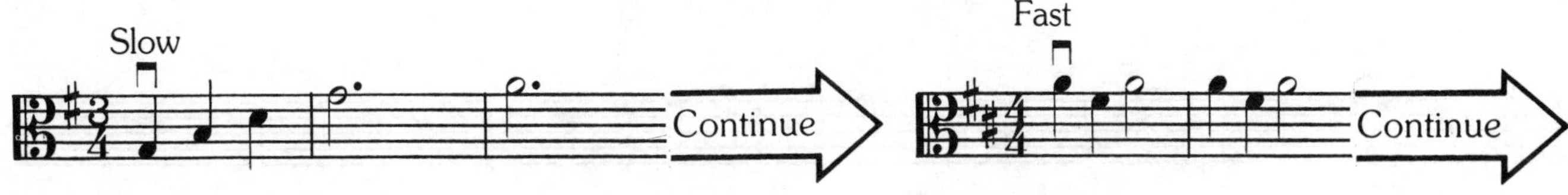

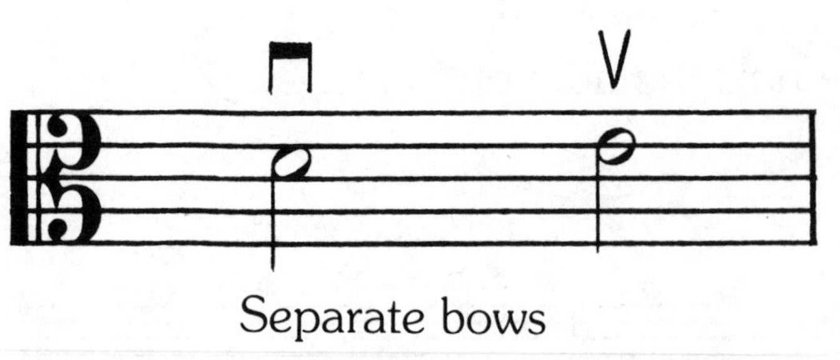

Scale of G

Etude

Ode to joy

From the Ninth Symphony

LUDWIG VAN BEETHOVEN
(1770-1827)

The wizard

1st and 2nd-time bars

The nightingale

Bonjour!

Allegro

Jingle bells

Presto

American traditional

The first Nowell

Joyfully

English traditional carol

O come, all ye faithful

Moderato

(Accompaniment)

J.F. WADE (1711-1786)

O little town of Bethlehem

Moderato

(Accompaniment)

English traditional carol

Dynamics

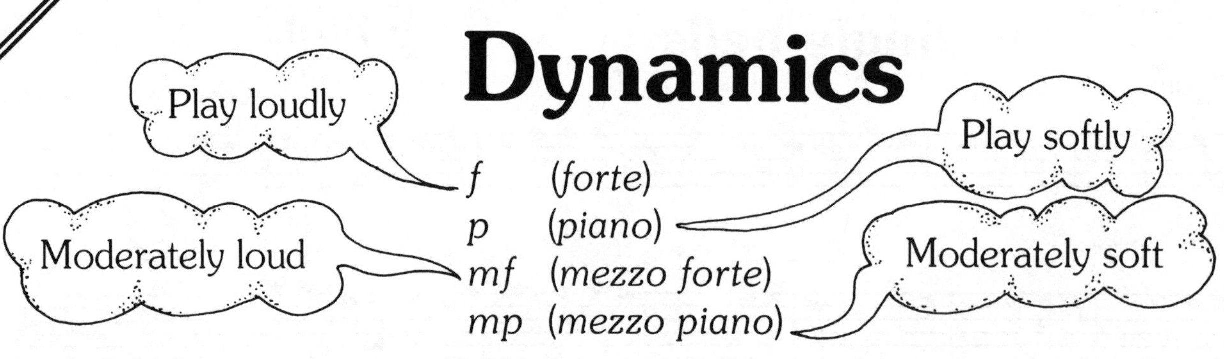

Echoes

Allegretto

f *p* *f* *p*

f *p* *f* *p*

Frère Jacques

French traditional

Brightly

Round

(1) *f* *p* (2) *f* *p* (3) *f* *p* (4) *f* *p*

The willow tree

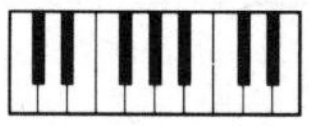

Flowing

mp

mf *mp*

Pattern

Moderato

mf

phrase A | phrase B | phrase A repeated | phrase C

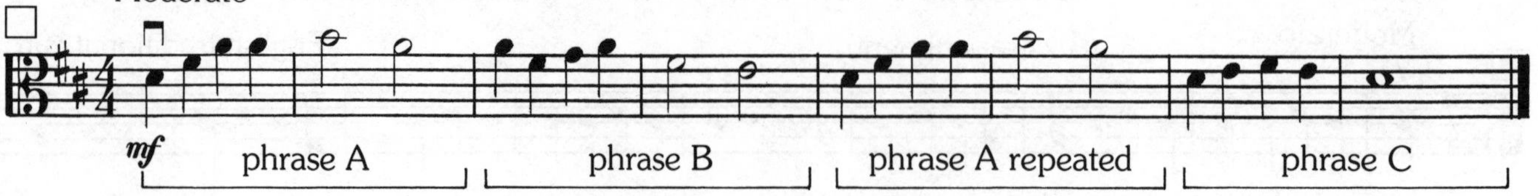

Compose a piece with the same structure as 'Pattern'

Tied notes

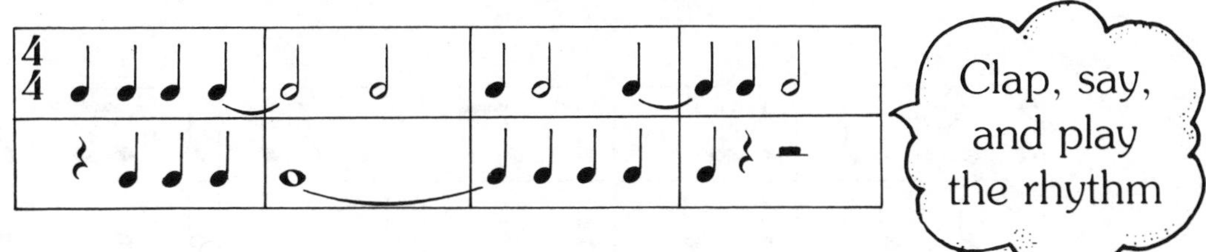

Clap, say, and play the rhythm

A minimin tied to a crotchet lasts for 3 beats 

A crotchet tied to a crotchet lasts for 2 beats 

A semibreve tied to a crotchet lasts for 5 beats, and so on 

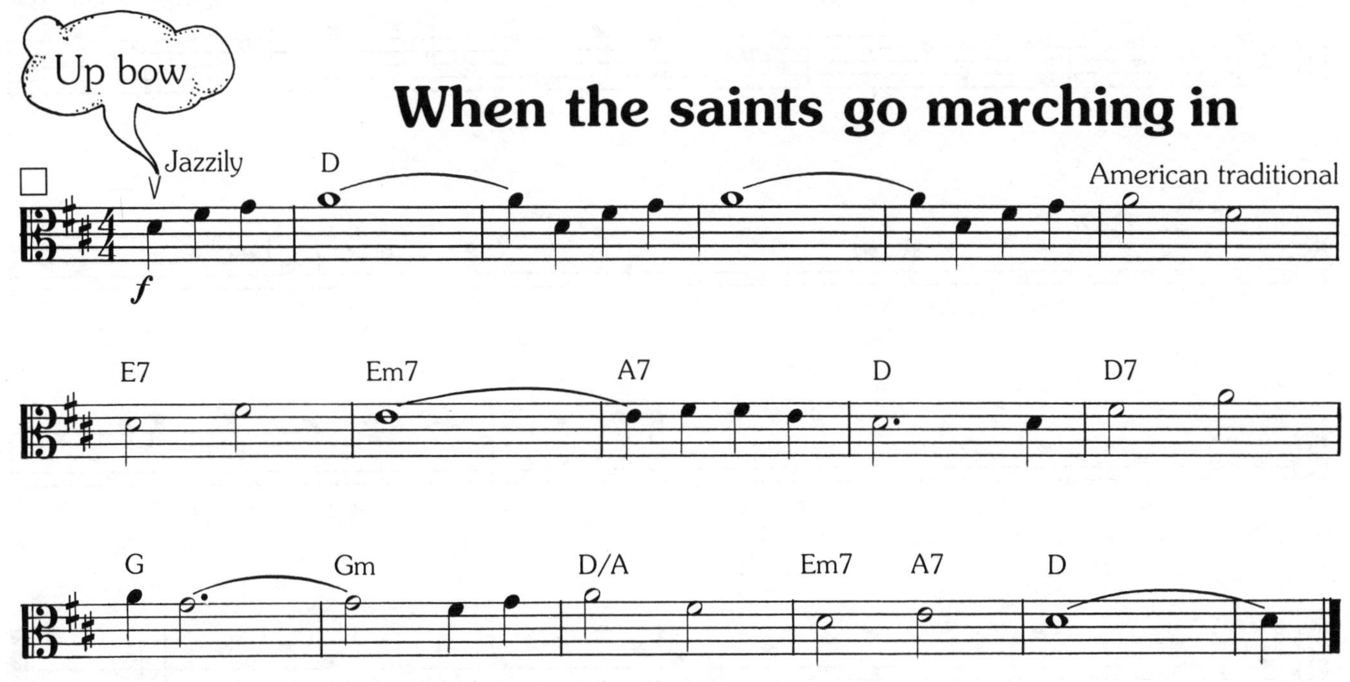

Syncopation

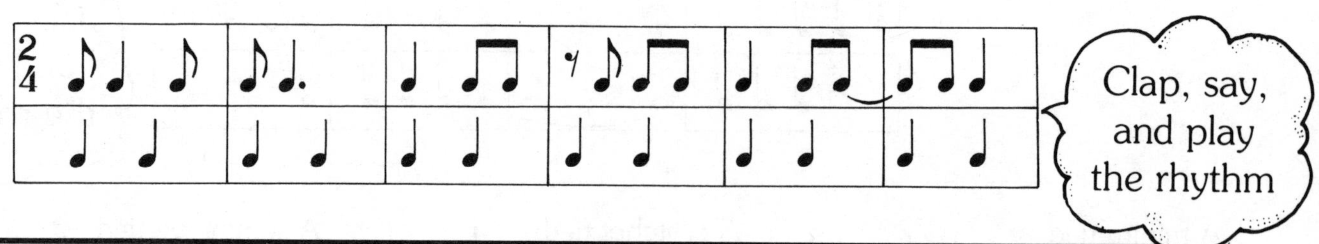

The rolling heather

Moderato

Scottish traditional

p

Twelve bar blues

Jazzily

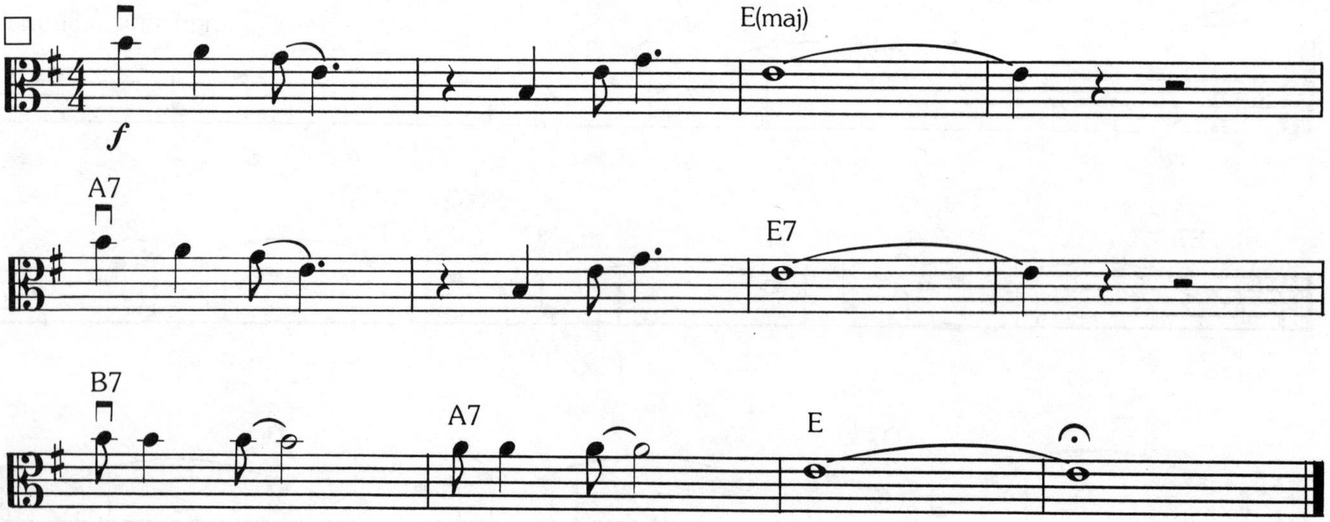

Em

E(maj)

f

A7

E7

B7

A7

E

Jamaican dance

Traditional

Sing a rainbow

Words and Music by ARTHUR HAMILTON

Semplice

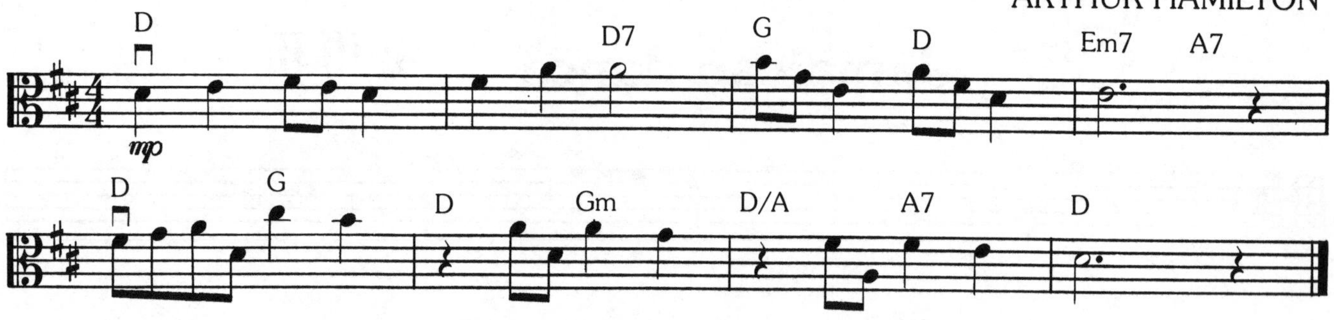

D D7 G D Em7 A7

D G D Gm D/A A7 D

Sam's piece

Composed by thirteen-year old Sam Wilkinson

Allegro

The white cliffs of Dover

Words by WALTER KENT
Music by NAT BURTON

Sentimentally

A7 D F♯m D7 G G♯° D/A Bm Em7

A A7 D Bm Em7 A7 D F♯m D7 G G♯°

D/A Bm Em7 A A7 D G D D7

G G+ Em/G G♯° D/A D D7 G Em

Bm Bm E7 Em7 A7 D F♯m D7

G G♯° D/A Bm Em7 A A7 D B♭ D

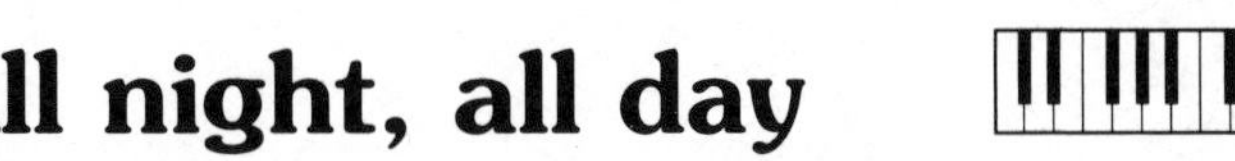

All night, all day

Spiritual

In 5/4 time each bar adds up to five crotchet beats
The clowns
Composed by thirteen-year old Collette Cassidy
Giocoso
Fine
f
D.C. al Fine
I gave my love a cherry
Traditional
Andante cantabile
mf
Passion chorale
JOHANN SEBASTIAN BACH
(1685-1750)
Religioso
mp

Old Macdonald

Traditional

The key of G major

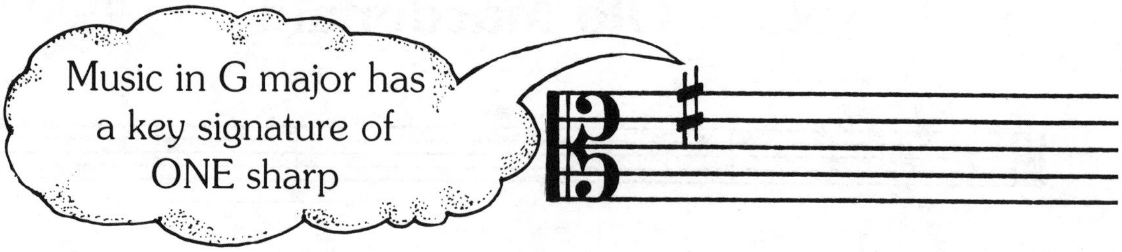

Music in G major has a key signature of ONE sharp

This C is written above one leger line. It is played with '2nd finger back'

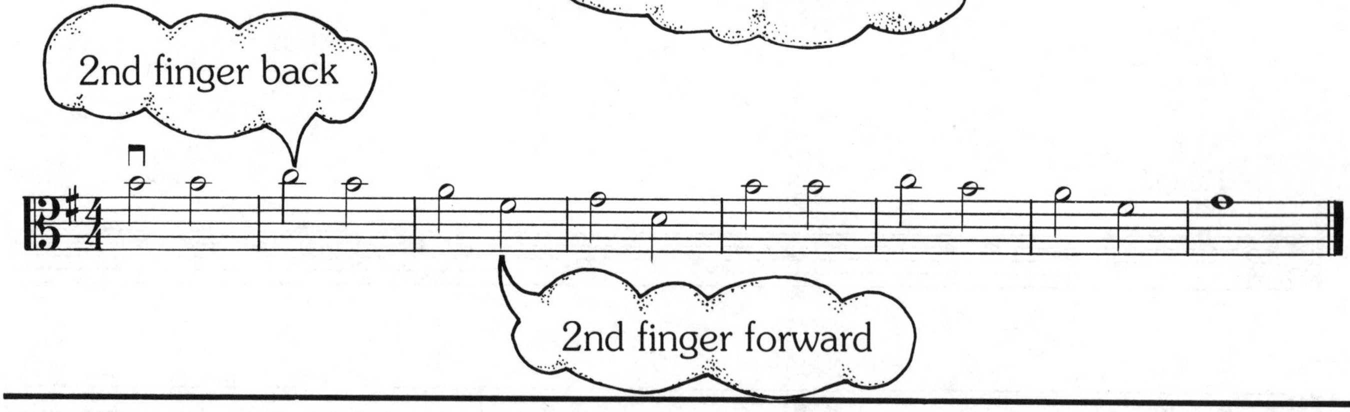

2nd finger back

2nd finger forward

Love me tender

Words and Music by VERA MATSON and ELVIS PRESLEY

Valse

Yankee Doodle

American traditional

The grand old Duke of York

English traditional

Summer song

Czech traditional

Lullaby

Andante cantabile
Duet
COUNT 1 2 3 2 2 3
WHOLE BAR (or SEMIBREVE) rest
Up bow
O come, all ye faithful
Moderato
J.F. WADE (1711-1786)
Play by ear
Slowly
Continue
Brightly
Continue

Good King Wenceslas

English traditional carol

Accidentals

and its relationship with $\frac{2}{4}$ time.

$\frac{2}{4}$ means that each bar adds up to TWO CROTCHET BEATS

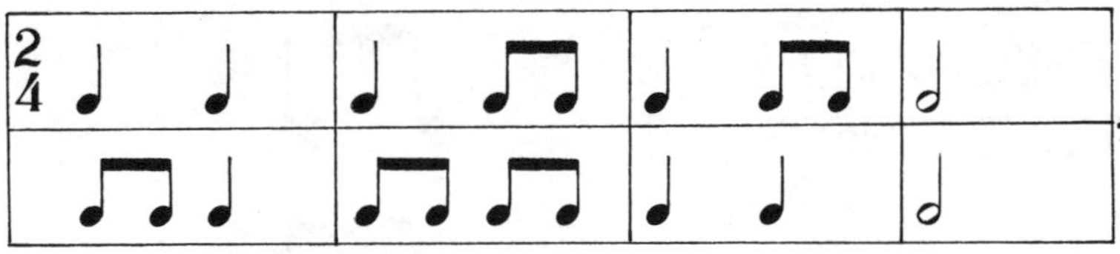

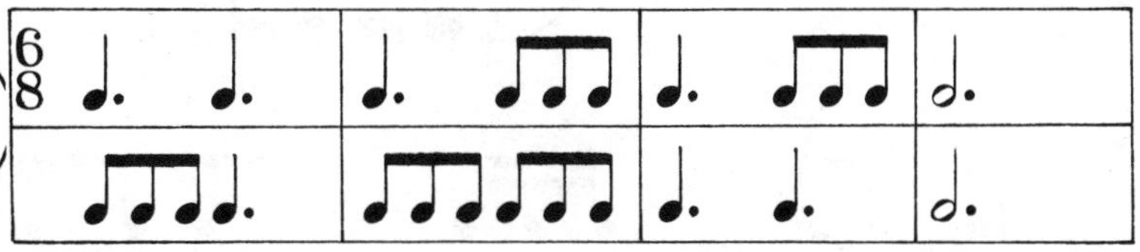

In $\frac{2}{4}$ time quavers are grouped in twos, to make up ONE CROTCHET BEAT

Clap, say, and play the rhythm

$\frac{6}{8}$ time means each bar adds up to TWO DOTTED CROTCHET BEATS

In $\frac{6}{8}$ time quavers are grouped in threes to make up ONE DOTTED CROTCHET BEAT

Irish jig

Traditional

Con Brio

f

Pop goes the weasel

English traditional

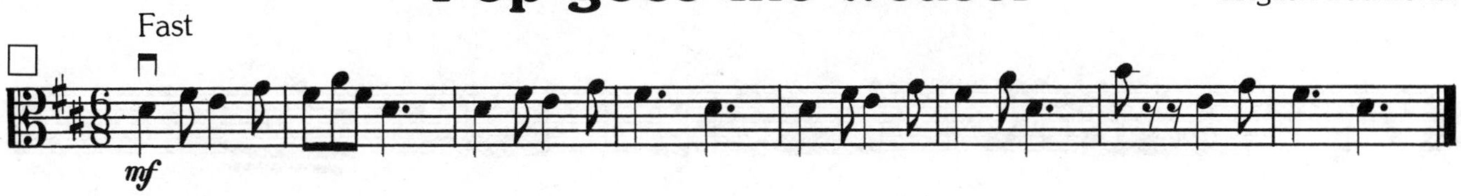

Fast

mf

Semiquavers

Dotted quavers

Happy birthday to you

Words and Music by
PATTY S. HILL and MILDRED HILL

Oh Susannah

American traditional

Brightly

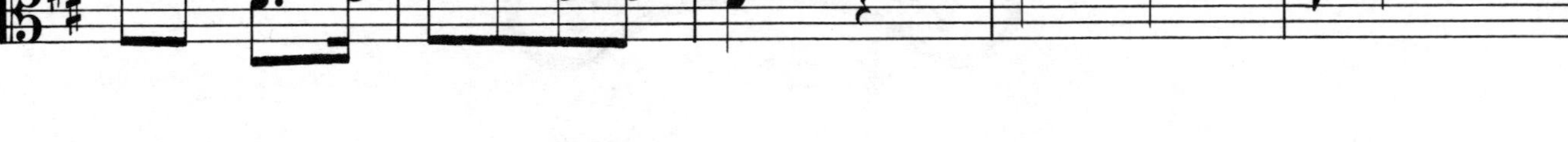

TWO MINIM BEATS in each bar

Chitty Chitty Bang Bang

Words and Music by
RICHARD SHERMAN and ROBERT SHERMAN

Allegro

Scarboro' fair

Traditional

Liltingly

Happily

Allegro

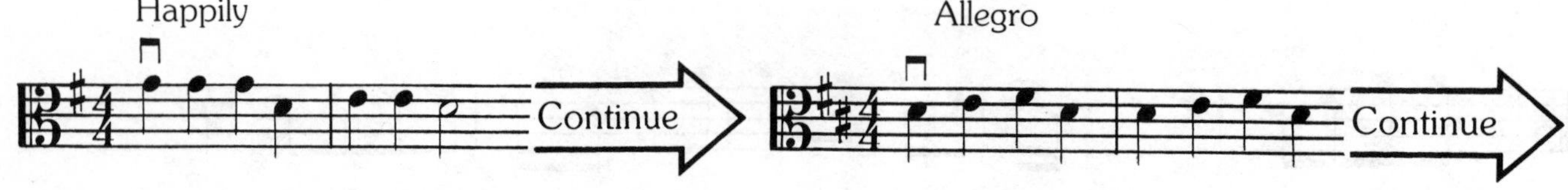

The QUAVER TRIPLET means that three quavers are played in the time of one crotchet

Amazing grace

Traditional

Slowly

1.

mp

Slurring three notes to a bow

Ruthin gardens

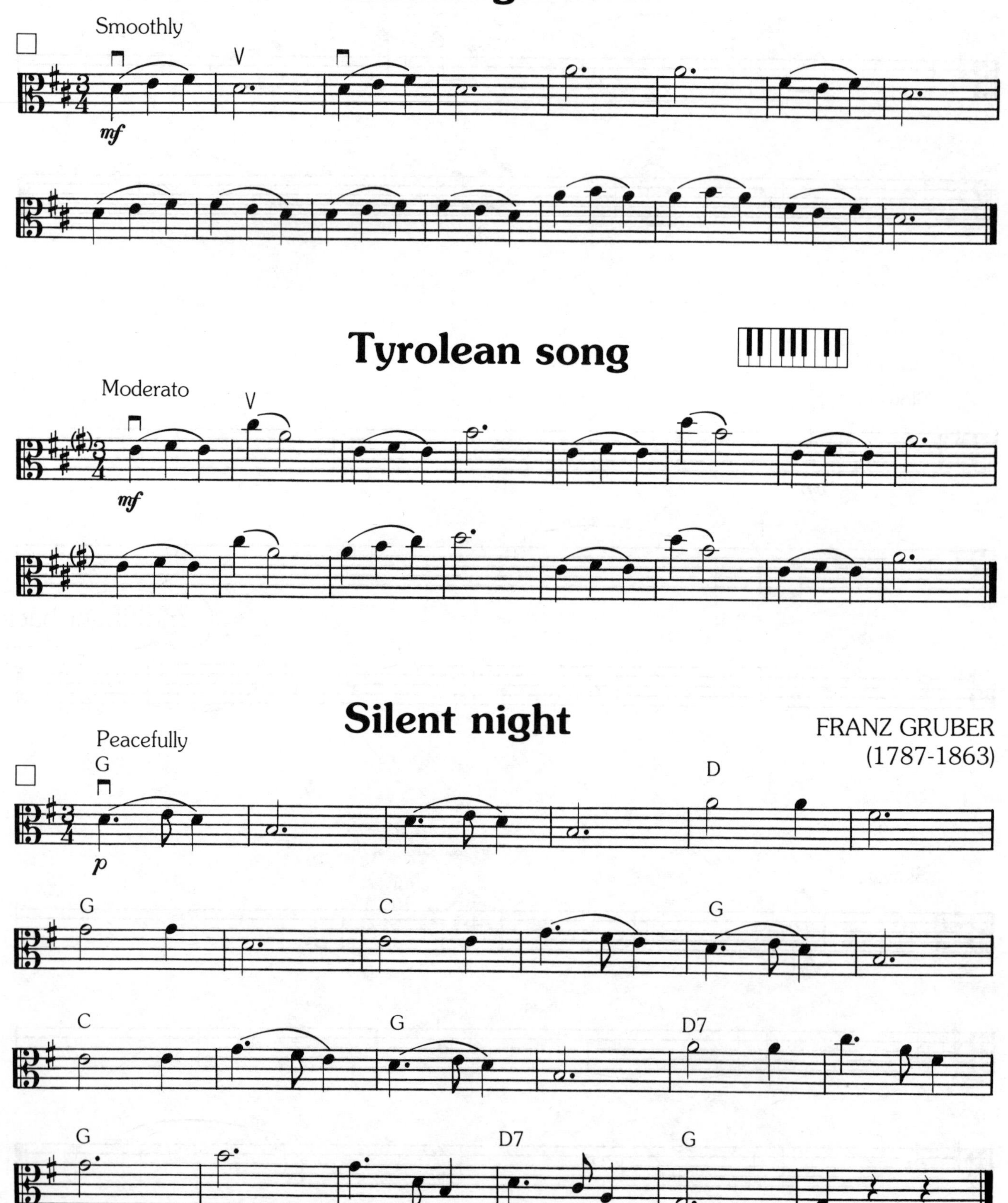

The Skye boat song

Scottish traditional

Smoothly

1.

mf

(𝄐) Fine

f

D. C. al Fine
(no repeat)

rit.

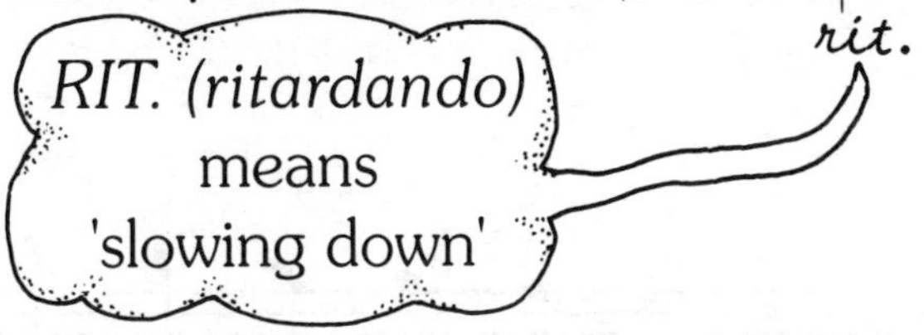

RIT. (ritardando) means 'slowing down'

Smoothly

2.

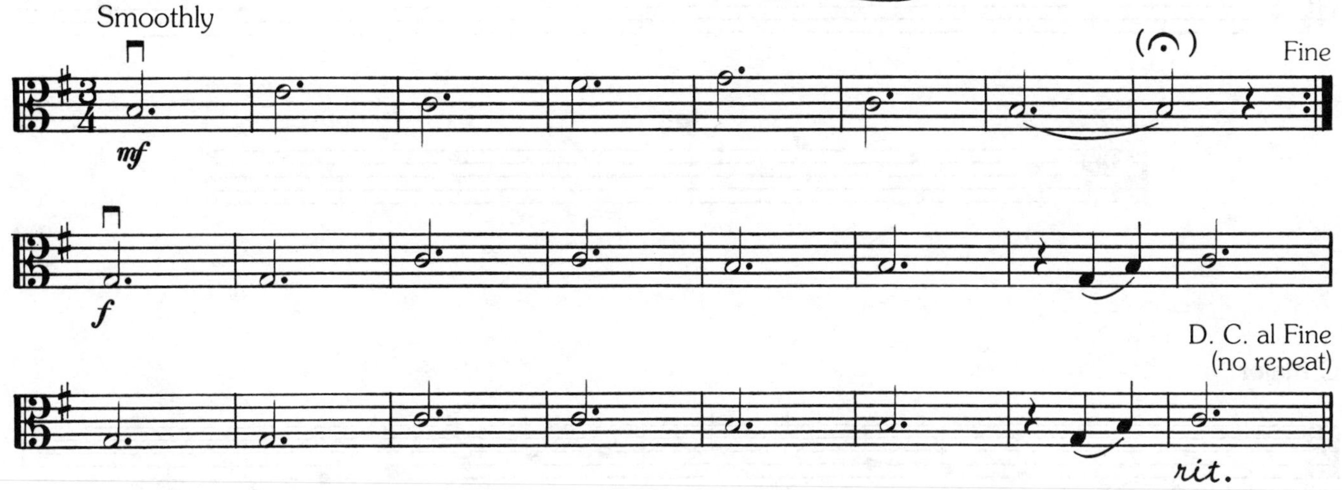

mf

(𝄐) Fine

f

D. C. al Fine
(no repeat)

rit.

Scales and arpeggios

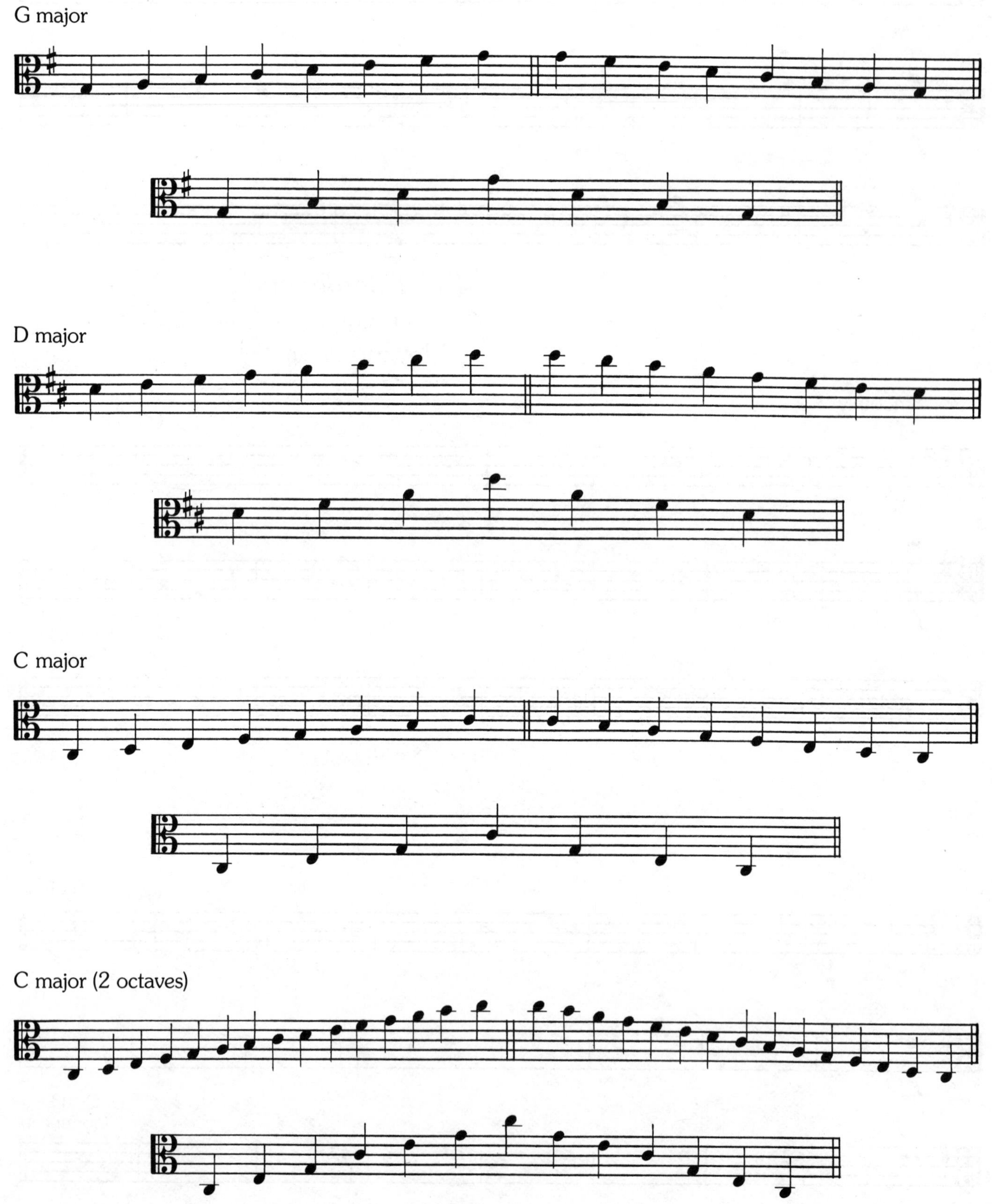